OLD BRIDGEND
IN PHOTOGRAPHS

1 The 'new bridge' seen from the old, original 15th-century stone bridge. The building overhanging the river on the left is Bridge House, now demolished. The bridge was erected in 1821, with the construction of Park Street, as part of the scheme to 'avoid the stupendous Newcastle Hill'. This bridge was used from the 1830s by the mail coach. It was demolished in 1912 and replaced by the present structure

OLD BRIDGEND IN PHOTOGRAPHS

with a foreword and commentaries by
D. Glyn Williams

STEWART WILLIAMS

Barry

First published in July 1978
© Stewart Williams, Publishers,
Bryn Awel, Buttrills Road, Barry,
South Glamorgan

ISBN 0 900807 30 X

Printed in Wales by D. Brown & Sons Ltd., Bridgend

Foreword

IN WRITING OF his native town of Bridgend, H. J. Randall referred to it as one following no general pattern. 'It is a town of anomalies and peculiarities. Although it was the market centre of a productive district, it never became a borough; it never owned its own town hall; it never possessed town walls . . . But of all its peculiarities the most striking and significant is its geographical location'. That location is on the river Ogmore at the western end of the fertile Vale of Glamorgan and is the natural focal point for the industrial valleys of Garw, Llynfi and Ogmore. Unlike so many other former counties, Glamorgan could not lay claim to a county town. Bridgend, however, might have advanced a justifiable claim to be so regarded for it fulfils many desiderata of a county town. Situated in the centre of Glamorgan, every place in the county, with the exception of the Gower peninsula, can be easily reached from it.

For hundreds of years the town has been recognised as the obvious market place of a productive region. It had a weekly market in Elizabethan times, a fact noted by the famous antiquary Rice Merrick. This proud distinction was lost, however, when the centuries-old market was transferred to Cowbridge in March, 1977.

North and south of the river Ogmore, which flows through Bridgend, the floor of the valley is fairly broad, but at the site of the town it narrows to a gap that is almost a gorge. Between the high ground of Newcastle, with its church and castle, and Brackla Hill on the eastern side, there was a ford of supreme excellence. It was the hub of tracks and paths radiating in all directions and the recognised means of communication between the hamlets of Oldcastle and Newcastle.

It has been surmised that 1425 was the date of the building of a four-arched stone bridge at the northern end of the ford. With the completion of the bridge the town became an entity rather than two separate small hamlets on each side of the river. It is thought that the town took its name from the old bridge which still stands as a two-arched structure, the result of two of the original arches being swept away in one of the many floods which have assailed the town. The use of the old bridge is now confined to pedestrians only. Five centuries after it was built the local authority,

seeking a new coat of arms, selected the bridge to appear on the shield and adopted as the motto a proverb from the ancient Welsh tales of the Mabinogion, 'A vo penn bit pont' (He who would be a leader, let him be a bridge).

From the fifteenth to the nineteenth centuries the town's growth was slow and unspectacular. References to it in documents are few but those which do appear are not without significance. The importance and economic position of the town are recognised by the evidence of the market being one of the busiest in the county. The pace of life quickened when the effects of the Industrial Revolution were felt. The small rural community was on the threshold of tremendous changes which were to transform its character. A large three-storey building to house a woollen factory was erected to the north of the bridge on land which fronts the main road to Tondu. It was hoped that by manufacturing textiles the export of raw wool to places outside the county would be prevented. The enterprise failed and subsequently after a spell as a tanyard the building was converted into a brewery, and so it remained until this century when it was demolished and a modern warehouse for a large brewing company was built on the site.

In the second quarter of the last century the foundations of a modern town were laid. This was the period of building and expansion. A new three-arched bridge was built across the river some 100 yards upstream from the fifteenth-century bridge and a road was constructed along the present Park Street to avoid the fearsome Newcastle Hill. Ten years later a new road was built from Brocastle at the foot of Crack Hill to Bridgend. This enabled coaches which hitherto had travelled via Corntown and Ewenny to Laleston and the west to go through the town for the first time. The construction of the Dyffryn Llynfi — Porthcawl tramroad brought a demand for railway facilities in Bridgend. Within a year or two of the completion of the track to Porthcawl a meeting was held at Bridgend 'to consider the expediency of forming a branch railroad from the Dyffryn Llynfi Railroad near a place called the Miners Arms to the town of Bridgend'. The undertaking was completed and the Bridgend Railway, as it became known, was opened in the latter part of 1830. A commemorative plaque marking the terminus in Bridgend can be seen on the wall adjoining the premises of Messrs. Evans & Phillips in Quarella Road.

Some 200 yards along the tramroad from this terminus a new workhouse was built by the Guardians of Bridgend and Cowbridge Union of parishes. The original building of 1836-7 still exists being part of the town's General Hospital complex. Twenty years later a lunatic asylum was built at Angelton two miles outside the town. Both institutions have been the subject of cruel jokes and for many years the term 'Bridgend' was synonymous with lunacy in the opinion of many ill-informed people. Happily, we are more enlightened in our approach to mental illness nowadays and the stigma attached to hospitals provided for the treatment and cure of nervous and mental disorders has disappeared. A general improvement in the financial status of individuals during the past century has rendered unnecessary the workhouse with all its heavy Victorian overtones of ill-treatment and cruelty.

By the middle of the last century steam locomotives were seen in South Wales and on 18 June 1850 the first steam-driven train halted at the present railway station amidst great rejoicing. Bridgend's visionaries had realised a dream that the town should be included on the main railway line from the West of England to Swansea. Railways from the town to the three coal-bearing valleys, and subsequently to the coal-exporting port of Barry, were provided in the second half of the century. The first of these, to the Llynfi Valley, effectively sealed the fate of the tramroad.

The great controversy surrounding the preservation or demolition of the Town Hall will be fresh in the minds of many of the town's inhabitants. This is the building which in 1845 replaced the 'old' Town Hall of which little is known. The new Town Hall will be remembered as a large edifice whose massive pillars appeared to dominate Dunraven Place. It was a tribute to civic pride that more than three quarters of its total cost was met by public subscription. In many respects it was a tragedy that the local authority was not responsible for the Hall as the building was sadly in need of maintenance and repair work for which no funds were available from the Trust, the controlling body. The building was demolished in 1971.

When the old Town Hall was pulled down in 1843 the general market, which had transacted business beneath the upper room, transferred in accordance with the Bridgend Market Act, 1836 'to a very commodious market place on the site of the old tennis court ground . . .' In 1837 a new market was opened and remained on this site (between Caroline Street and Queen Street) until its demolition in 1971 after which it rose again as part of the town development plan.

Without exception the late nineteenth-century commentators refer to Bridgend as 'a thriving town' and evidence to support this claim abounds in contemporary records of the transformation of the town during this period.

In the early decades of the twentieth century traffic congestion within the town necessitated the building of a new concrete-reinforced bridge to replace the 1821 structure, and the construction of a by-pass road from Waterton to Laleston. Many will recall the opening in 1938 of the Royal Ordnance Factory, known to all as the Arsenal, on the outskirts of the town. With the end of the Second World War the factory was converted into an industrial estate. Immediately opposite the northern end of the estate the Waterton Trading Estate has been developed in recent years. By 1979 'Ford' will have a different connotation in Bridgend when a brand new factory commences production of car engines, thus giving the town's economy a massive boost.

Fame and notoriety came in equal measure to the town in March 1945 when sixty-seven German Officers escaped through a tunnel from Island Farm P.O.W. camp alongside the main A48 road. It took a week to recapture them and made history as the biggest break-out from a British P.O.W. camp in the Second World War.

The Gorsedd circle of stones in the lovely Newbridge Fields is a constant reminder of the only visit of the Royal National Eisteddfod of Wales to the town in 1948, eight years later than scheduled.

Even as the 'thriving town' developed in the last century, so does it stretch its boundaries today. Work on the development of the Brackla Site and proposals for future growth in the industrial and housing sectors will ensure that the Bridgend of the future will maintain, if not enhance, its long-held reputation as the leading town in Mid Glamorgan.

Looking out at us from these pages are places and faces, scenes and occasions, which have been a small part of the history of Bridgend over a period of some 75 years. They illustrate the importance and value of recording our local history, in this case through the camera lens, but equally so in words and through projects, exhibitions, lectures and so forth. In this latter respect Bridgend is fortunate in having a local history society whose own history is well worth recording and, incidentally, whose example has inspired this volume.

The society was formed at a meeting in March 1952 at the Civic Restaurant (now part of the Post Office premises) in Derwen Road and attended by about 100 townsfolk, among them local historians and chroniclers of the calibre of Thomas Bevan, John Lewis, Edward Loveluck, Aeron Price, D. J. Price, H. J. Randall, W. M. Rees and Roderick Williams. We are all debtors to the past, and to these men in particular, whose individual and collective contributions to our knowledge of the town and district were considerable. Regrettably, little of their work survives in published form, apart from H. J. Randall's scholarly work and Thomas Bevan's contributions to *Glamorgan Historian*.

Their influence in the formation and development of the local history society soon became apparent. A committee was appointed and decided upon a programme of lectures during the six months of autumn and winter with proposals for summer excursions and visits to places of interest. From this pattern there has been little deviation over the years. The first chairman was H. J. Randall (later elected president), with Thomas Bevan as his deputy, D. J. Price, hon. secretary, and Albert Hesling, hon. treasurer. An approach was made to the Glamorgan Education Authority for the use of the lecture room at the Technical College (now the College of Technology) and this subsequently became the permanent meeting place of the society.

On 9 April 1952 the first meeting of the newly-formed society was held at which Dr. Dilwyn John, Director of the National Museum of Wales, spoke on 'The museum in relation to local history'. It set a standard which has been maintained down the years and has resulted in the forging of valuable links with the National Museum, the Extra Mural Department of University College, Cardiff, and Glamorgan Record Office. A list of the many lecturers reads like a 'Who's Who'. Well known names abound and their willingness to visit Bridgend must certainly have been due to the reputation of many of the society's founder members. Of exceptional interest was the visit in October 1966 of a local man who achieved national prominence as the Keeper of Public Records, Sir David Evans, O.B.E., D.Litt., who spoke on 'Public Records in Wales'.

Members' nights were introduced to the programme of winter sessions in the formative years of the society and have given individual members an opportunity to air their specialised knowledge, thus creating a renewed awareness of the rich traditions of the district. Since 1964-65 the late Thomas Bevan (acting secretary for a session) and Dr. Doreen Annear (the present hon. secretary) have done a great service by providing summaries in its business records of all lectures given to the society. Without this information it would be difficult to discover the infinite variety and scope of topics presented.

Many years before conservation of the environment was recognised as a responsibility of all civilised communities, members of the society were expressing their concern at the lack of thought and feeling for the past as revealed in the development of areas of Mid Glamorgan in the interests of industry. In 1957 Mr. Denis Verity, a prominent member, referred to the fact that in the vicinity of the site of Kenfig Castle industrial development necessitating the removal of sand and the siting of railway and marshalling yards was in progress. Three years later the same member directed attention to the imminent demolition of the town's provision market and suggested that the ancient clock bell and brick columns should be preserved in the new market building. Subsequently the society were informed that the Urban District Council had already earmarked the articles for preservation.

The society's first exhibition was held during the town's civic festival week in September 1973. It coincided with their 21st anniversary and at the opening the president, Albert Hesling, expressed the hope that the display would be the forerunner of many and would provide a basis for the ultimate goal — a museum of local history in Bridgend. This has remained a primary objective, but despite the herculean efforts of Dr. Annear and society members, the goodwill of the authorities and examination of several possible locations, none of which unfortunately proved suitable, it remains a dream which hopefully will be realised one day.

To mark its 21st anniversary the society held a celebration dinner to which the present writer was invited as their guest. It was fitting that Mrs. D. J. Price, widow of the 'inimitable first secretary' and the one remaining life member, responded to the toast proposed to 'The Society'. Four years later the mood for celebration continued when the Jubilee Dinner was held in May 1977 to end the 25th session. Two old and faithful friends of the society, Patricia and Donald Moore, attended as guests, and an appeal was made by the new chairman Mr. David J. Pearce, for the society to take a more active role in recording anecdotes and reminiscences of the older inhabitants of the town and district in the pursuit of local history.

Inevitably time has taken its toll of the founders, but they are remembered with gratitude and tangibly in the case of Thomas Bevan whose name is perpetuated in the Memorial Prize awarded annually for original research undertaken by pupils in Bridgend Grammar (now Comprehensive) Schools. The result has been an interesting series of essays ranging from 'Education in Bridgend' (Miss Eleanor Harries), 'Road systems of Bridgend from the Bronze Age to the present day' (D. Knights), 'South Crop — the industrial history of the southern outcropping of coal in South Wales' (S. K. Roberts) to 'Bridgend Station and the railways of Bridgend (I. D. Mundy). Out of the society's enthusiasm to 'spread the gospel' was born the idea for this book of photographs which it is hoped will give a closer insight into the life and times of the old market town over a period which has seen some dramatic changes.

The Town

2 The old bridge, built *c*.1425, which marked the foundation of the town and, it is claimed, gave the town its name. Originally it was a four-arched structure with steep approaches on both sides. It survived the elements until 1775 when, during the August flood, two arches on the Newcastle side were swept away. They were replaced by a single arch

3 Wesley Church and the beginnings of Tondu Road, with Newcastle in the background, seen from the 'new bridge' *c*.1900

4 The approach to Court Road with the Police Station and Magistrates' Court on the left, the Randall memorial right of centre, and the then Cottage Hospital, *c*.1902

5 In the foreground is the Cattle Market with The Green alongside. Left background is Brackla Quarry in front of which is the Railway Station and its approach. The large building in right background is Hermon Chapel, built 1862. View taken *c*.1906

6 Coity Road toll-house converted into a shop. It is the only surviving toll-house in the town. Some years ago a lorry collided with the entrance and demolished part of the original house

7/8 These were among the last of the old cottages etc. of the Rhiw before their demolition and the subsequent redevelopment of the area. The Rhiw would have been one of the earliest tracks leading to the river ford used by travellers bound for Newcastle and beyond

9/10/11 Three photographs, all taken from a spot outside the present J. & A. Furnishers, which depict the development of one of the main shopping thoroughfares — Nolton Street. In the first the semi-rural character and the beginning of the growth of the town are revealed. By 1963 shops have replaced trees and shrubs, the Dunraven Estate Offices are clearly seen, and the highest point of the facade of Nolton Presbyterian Chapel is visible behind the offices. In 1973 the entrance to the Rhiw Arcade had been built and the days of the Chapel were numbered. Soon it was replaced by Ogwr Borough Council Information Offices

12 The junction of Caroline Street and Queen Street in 1900. The large building on the left, known as Davies's Buildings, then accommodated the Post Office

13 Caroline Street *c.*1906-7 looking towards the Cottage Hospital from Dunraven Place. The Provision Market, seen middle right, had not long been covered in

14 Caroline Street *c.*1916. The premises of Bevan & Lloyd, grocers, were later occupied for many years by W. H. Smith & Son, Ltd.

15 Caroline Street as it looked in the early 1920s with a few motor vehicles contrasting sharply with the horse traffic in the other views on these pages

16 The former High Street in the early years of the 20th century. It is surprising how many buildings have remained unchanged during the past seventy years

17 Parking was no problem in Dunraven Place *c.*1920. The three modes of transport present a picture of tranquillity long since forgotten!

18 In the expanding town of the 1840s there was a great need for a hall large enough to hold public meetings and·courts. The new or second Town Hall was the outcome. Completed in 1844, the building was erected for a contract price of £1,450. The cost, except for £350 from county funds, was met by voluntary donations. The hall was used for a variety of purposes — entertainments, banquets, concerts, dramatic performances, political meetings and meetings of the townspeople. Sadly the changed pattern of society after the Second World War robbed the building of much of its usefulness. As a result the structure fell into disrepair and became, so it was claimed, a danger to passers-by. Following a proposal to demolish the hall, a long battle was fought to retain it, but the preservationists lost the day and the building disappeared in 1971

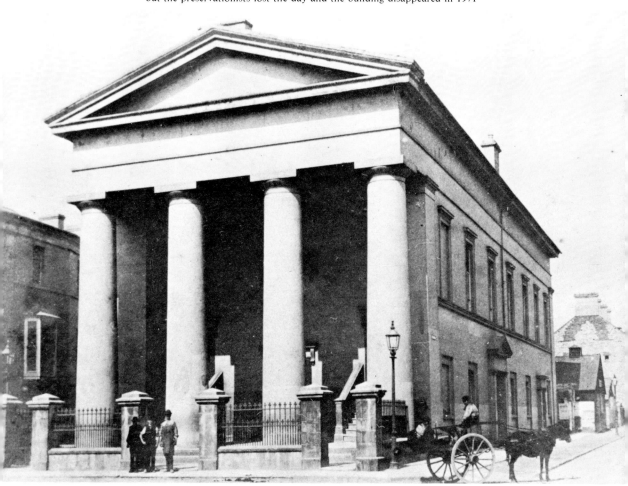

19/20 Two of the buildings occupied by the Post Office. (Above) Davies's Buildings, *c*.1900 and (below) the more familiar building at the top of Court Road/Station Hill, built in 1926. This latter building carries a preservation order and serves as sorting offices following the removal of the main Post Office to Wyndham House (where once stood the Town Hall) in July 1976

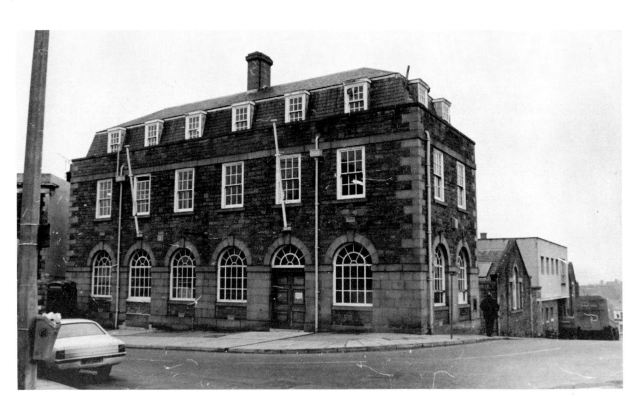

21 The reinforced concrete bridge which replaced the 1821 structure. On the tablet affixed to the pillar appears an inscription recording the opening of the bridge on 12 July, 1912

22 The former Provision Market with its two entrances from Caroline Street. A number of the shops bearing names familiar to older inhabitants have gone and been replaced by a large branch of Boots and a new arcade

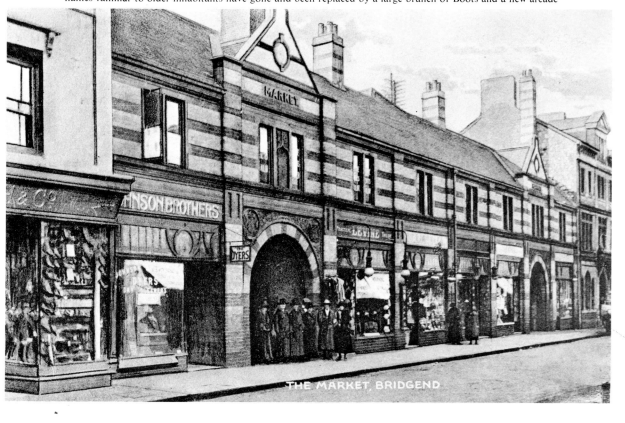

23/24 Two views of Nolton Street, *c.*1921. (Above) the railings on the left enclose Nolton Church Institute on the site of which can now be found J. & A. Furnishers. The Singer sewing machine sign has disappeared, but the shop remains in the same premises today. (Below) the delivery of petrol is to the pump belonging to Board's garage. The entrance to the Rhiw is immediately behind the small knot of men on the left

25 The 'top' end of Nolton Street, *c.*1900. Except for changes in tenancies and trades the shops on the left appear to be little different from those of today

26 The public weighbridge in Wyndham Street opposite both the *Railway Inn* and *Dunraven Arms* on a site now occupied by a small traffic island. The weighbridge was subsequently removed to Derwen Road. The character in the photograph is Mr. John Howe who was employed as check-weigher

27 This 15th-century house on Newcastle Hill is known as the Old Hospice. It is owned by the Priory for Wales of the Order of St. John. There was a theory that the building was a hospice of the Knights of St. John, but this has been disproved by historians

28 These cottages, bounding the Square, Newcastle Hill, make up one of the oldest parts of the town. All, except for the shop and neighbouring cottage, are now disused

29 A view across the town looking towards Newcastle from the Brackla Quarry, *c*.1910

30 The top end of Park Street in 1910. A present-day photograph would reveal little if any grass and woodland

31 Taken in September 1929 this aerial view of the town centre emphasises the tremendous changes which have since taken place. On the roughly triangular piece of land (bottom left) the Embassy cinema and car park now stand. Still on the left of the photograph, across the river the Cattle Market occupies the site of the present Bus Station. At the Park Street end of the bridge, Bridge House has been removed, while part of the north side of Sunnyside and the 'pop' factory have made way for the inner by-pass road. The allotments too are no more

32 In 1900 this was the view from Park fields looking towards St. Mary's Church, Nolton. Roads, houses and a large Recreation Centre now cover the fields

33 Adare Street looking south-east in the days when car parking was allowed on each side of the road, but on alternate days

Transport

34 This Handley Page bomber must have created a mighty stir when it landed on Coity Fields in 1919. Among the crew was Flt. Lieut. R. H. (Bob) Thomas of Laleston who flew this magnificent machine in the First World War. The occasion was a victory-celebrating 'Round Britain Flight'. Bob can be seen third from the right in front of the aircraft

35 This aircraft, an Avro 504K, registered G-EBNH, was acquired in May 1927 by R. H. (Bob) Thomas, a prominent local businessman and proprietor of South Wales Airways (see plate 34). The photograph was taken in a field at Corntown which was used as a local base. In May 1928 the aircraft crashed near Bridgend

36 An early 20th-century shot of Bridgend Railway Station which was opened in June 1850 showing the G.W.R., Vale of Glamorgan and Valley lines

37 When motoring was a novelty and a pleasure. The location is the yard of the *Dunraven Arms*. In the background is the gable end of the *Railway Hotel*, with the name of the proprietor, W. W. Phillips, partly obscured. The building with the conical 'tower' is the studio of Ernest Carver (senr.)

38 Bridgend 'bus termini in the 1920s showing a Rhondda Tramways AEC saloon picking up passengers for Porthcawl. The land, which adjoined the Cattle Market, was used by several early 'bus operators who pioneered today's regular services between Bridgend, the Valleys and surrounding villages

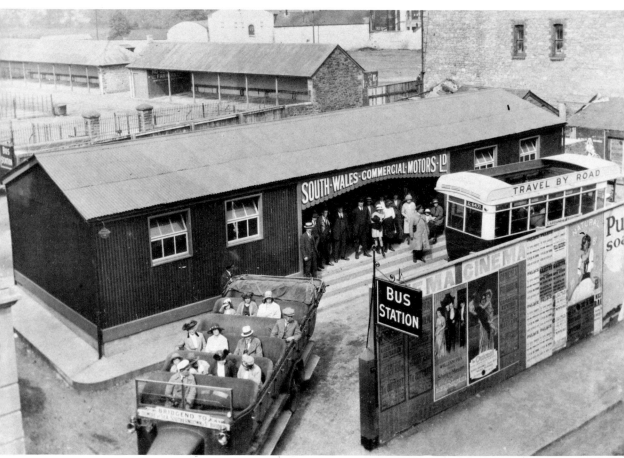

39 The first Bus Station in South Wales was opened in Market Street, Bridgend, in March 1922. A report in the trade press reported it as having 'ladies and general waiting room, bookstall, refreshment rooms, convenience for a wash and brush up, employees' messrooms and platforms for loading and unloading'. It cost £1,600. The Commer vehicles in the photograph operated on the Cardiff-Bridgend and Bridgend-Southerndown-St. Brides services

40 'Reliance', one of the small operators who ran between Bridgend, Ogmore-by-Sea and Southerndown. The company was owned by Thomas & Bennett, Greengate Garage, St. Brides. This photograph was taken *c.*1929

41 Out of 'Reliance' and Vale Motor Services emerged Green & White Services Ltd. in 1933. They provided a valuable link between Vale of Glamorgan villages and Bridgend. Western Welsh eventually took them over in 1938

42 Pencoed Motor Company Ltd., was formed in November 1933 to take over a number of 'bus operators on the Pencoed route. Their vehicle has pride of place in this 1935 photograph taken at the Bus Station

43/44 Charabanc outings were one of the more enjoyable features of the 1920s. Members of the local United Services Club and their ladies are here seen 'somewhere in Somerset'

45 In an era when there were comparatively few private cars, motor coach tours provided the means of visiting 'faraway places'. Even solid tyres did not diminish the pleasure

Sport, Entertainment and Social Occasions

46 According to press cuttings preserved by the descendants of Charles Verity, Bridgend Rugby Football Club was a thriving concern during the season 1878/79 and this is now regarded as the club's first season. A programme of events and functions to celebrate the club's centenary has already started. The committee for the 1939/40 season are seen here, among them the late W. J. Llewellyn (hon. secretary) and Glyn Hopkin (asst. hon. secretary)

47 Bridgend R.F.C. 1895. This team, captained by C. Williams, played on a field known as Five Bells Field or Warner's Field. This ground is now covered by Grove Road and Brynteg Avenue

48 Bridgend R.F.C. 1924/25. Captained by Cyril Thomas, the side contained one international, Daph Davies, who represented Wales on two occasions

49 Bridgend R.F.C. 1930/31. The background indicates that the side were playing on Coychurch Road ground. In the group are Willie Llewellyn, Welsh wing in the famous 1905 game against the All Blacks, W. J. Llewellyn, international referee and club secretary, and A. H. Jones, a member of the first Welsh XV to win at Twickenham in 1933

50 Bryntirion Preparatory School for Boys' Rugby XV 1928/29. Members of the staff include Rev. N. H. Parcell (Headmaster), I. W. R. North, G. W. Morgan and Glyn Thomas

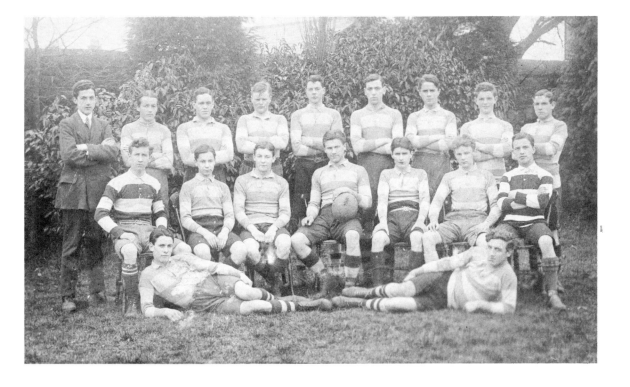

51/52 Rugby was played at Bridgend County School as far back as 1897 but the teams featured on this page are (above) the 1914 and (below) 1915 teams. During the period of the First World War few school matches were played

53 Bridgend County School Rugby XV 1925/26. This was a remarkable season with the team scoring 307 points and conceding 115 in 22 matches. Included in the XV is Idris Towill who won a junior international cap and went on to play in Rugby League football

54 Bridgend County School Rugby XV 1942/43. The war years were lean ones for rugby and all sport

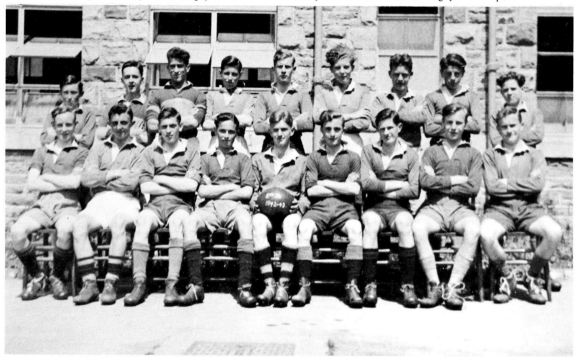

55 Bridgend Orient A.F.C. photographed at Angelton 1926/27. At this period the town had a number of soccer teams including the Stars, the Wednesdays — and even a team known as the 'Irish Lane Boys'

56 Glanrhyd Hospital A.F.C. winners of the Inter-Hospital Shield Competition 1949/50. The team also played in the Bridgend and District Amateur A.F. League

57 Older supporters of Glamorgan County Cricket Club will recognise many stalwarts of the side in its developing years. The household names of Maurice Turnbull, Jack Mercer, Arnold Dyson, Emrys and Dai Davies etc. appeared on the score card of this game played on the Coychurch Road Ground when a County XI met Bridgend in 1932. The game resulted in a draw, D. J. James taking six County wickets

58/59 The former Boys' County School had a proud record in athletics dating from the formation of the Glamorgan Secondary Schools AAA. At all levels the school's representatives have been winners on more than one occasion of the various cups. In the 1939 squad Dr Jack Matthews can be seen seated fourth from the right

60/61 A far cry from Kerry Packer and his World Series Cricket! (Above) the 'Bridgend C. XI 1894' containing some well-known names — Dr R. J. Moynan, Messrs T. D. Schofield, J. I. D. Nicholl, R. L. Knight etc. (Below) the town cricket team in 1902 on the occasion of a match at Newbridge Fields

62 Bridgend Cricket Club 1937. This team includes many players who gave years of sterling service to the club

63 Bryntirion Preparatory School for Boys. First XI *c.*1930

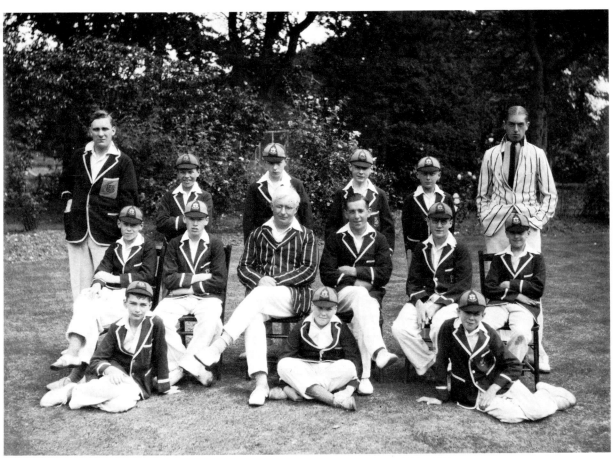

64 Bryntirion Preparatory School for Boys. Second XI *c.*1929

65 Bridgend County School cricket team 1915

66 Bridgend County School cricket team 1926. The side includes a number of boys — I. Towill, E. Evans etc. — who were prominent members of the rugby team

67 Bridgend County School cricket team 1928

68 Bridgend Hockey Team 1938 photographed at Brecon. Hockey in Bridgend dates back to 1896, soon after the game was introduced into South Wales

69 Parkfield Lawn Tennis Club *c*.1910. The club played on a 'beautiful ground beyond Sunnyside', *vide* a contemporary guide

70/71 Bridgend Bowling and Lawn Tennis Club 1920. The above photograph shows the tennis team with members of both the bowling and tennis clubs. Included in the photograph are Dr J. P. R. Williams' great-grandfather and grandfather. (Below) an overall view of courts and green

72/73 The unhurried activity of a game of bowls in 1920. The club had been formed in 1914 and occupied its present site overlooking the river and Newbridge Fields. (Below) the club pavilion which, in 1976, was completely destroyed by fire

THEATRE,
TOWN-HALL, BRIDGEND.

BY PARTICULAR DESIRE.

On WEDNESDAY, APRIL 14, 1841,

Will be presented Buxton's Comedy of

MARRIED LIFE,

Mr. Lyonel Lynx	Mr. H. JOHNSON.
Mr. Coddle	Mr. PLATT.
Mr. Samuel Dove	Mr. REID.
Mr. Younghusband	Mr. MERCER.
Mr. Dismal	Mr. MONTAGUE.
Mrs. Lyonel Lynx	Mrs. REID.
Mrs. Coddle	Mrs. PLATT.
Mrs. Samuel Dove	Mrs. SHEERER.
Mrs. Younghusband	Mrs. H. JOHNSON.
Mrs. Dismal	Miss SHEERER.

END OF THE COMEDY.

A COMIC SONG BY MR. REID.
A DUET BY MR. & MISS MERCER.

A SONG BY MR. MONTAGUE.

The whole to conclude with the Laughable Farce of

HIGH LIFE
BELOWSTAIRS

My Lord Duke	Mr. H. JOHNSON.
Sir Harry	Mr. MERCER.
Lovel	Mr. REID.
Phillip	Mr. MONTAGUE.
Thomas	Mr. PLATT.
Coachman	Mr. HEAL.
Lady Charlotte	Mrs. REID.
Lady Babb	Mrs. PLATT.
Kitty	Mrs. H. JOHNSON.
Cloe	Miss SHEERER.
Cook	Miss MERCER.

Prices of Admission—Boxes, 2s. 6d.—Front Seats, 2s.—Pit, 1s.
CHILDREN under Ten Years of Age, Half-Price.

Doors open at half-past SIX, and to commence at SEVEN o'Clock.
TICKETS to be had of Mr. H. JOHNSON.—WYNDHAM-ARMS, and of Mr. JOHN G. BIRD.

JOHN G. BIRD, PRINTER, &c., BRIDGEND.

74 References appear in a number of sources to the entertainment provided in the Town Hall. The date of the playbill shows the performance was given in the old building which was subsequently demolished to 'make way for the new'

THE FIRST WIRELESS CONCERT
IN BRIDGEND
HELD AT THE CAFE ROYAL
By C.H. BURGESS
58 SUNNYSIDE ROAD
5th MAR 1923.

75 The exciting early days of wireless broadcasting are captured in this photograph from March 1923. Similar groups gathered in many public places to hear the miracle of words and music in the air!

76 Cantatas and operettas were regular features of life in the early 1900s. Many of them were given by church and chapel choirs. The characters portrayed here were the parents of the donor and appeared in the cantata 'The Moabitess', a performance of which was given in the Town Hall, c.1910

77 This public presentation at the Town Hall in 1927 of 'H.M.S. Pinafore' by the Music and Dramatic Society of the former County School 'saw the highest peak of performance' of the society. A chorus of sixty, an excellent school orchestra and extremely talented actors combined to provide a memorable production. The conductor was Thomas Bevan, a member of the school staff and a local historian of no mean ability

78 A feature of many churches and chapels in the inter-war years was the Dramatic Society. The English Congregational Church, as it then was, was no exception. Calling themselves the Ogmorian Players, a full-length play, 'Aftermath', was produced and presented at the Town Hall in 1935. Written by C. Benson Roberts, seen standing in the centre immediately behind the settee, both play and production were highly praised

79 A brief interval of enjoyment in the sombre days of 1916. 'Fremans Red Cross Benefit . . . Aug 30, 1916' reads the chalked board. The location of the fair was The Green, now the Bus Station

80 The year of this 'great film sensation' was 1923

CINEMA BRIDGEND
FOR SIX DAYS
Commencing MONDAY, SEPTEMBER 17.

THE Great Film Sensation.

DR. MABUSE

The Great Unknown

15,000 Feet of Mystery & Sensation

Special Augmented Orchestra
In attendance.

PLEASE NOTE—Doors open 5.30 p.m.
Commence Prompt at 6 p.m.
COME EARLY TO SECURE YOUR SEATS
NO INCREASE IN PRICES.

IMPERIAL PRINTING CO., CARDIFF.

The House of Granger
Presents
The Film Sensation
"DR MABUSE"
The Great Unknown.

THEATRE,
TOWN-HALL, BRIDGEND.

UNDER THE PATRONAGE OF A
PARTY OF LADIES.

FOR THE BENEFIT OF
MRS. REID.

On FRIDAY, APRIL 16th, 1841,

When will be presented, the admired Pathetic Drama (in Three Acts) entitled

THERESE,
OR, THE ORPHAN OF GENEVA.

Carwin	Mr. H. JOHNSON.	Fontaine	Mr. PLATT.
Count	Mr. MERCER.	Lavigne	Mr. MONTAGUE.
Picard	Mr. HEAL.	Magistrate	Mr. HENRY.
Therese (the Orphan of Geneva)	Mrs. REID.	Countess	Mrs. PLATT.
Dame Bridget	Miss SHEERER.	Nannette	Miss MERCER.

ACT 1. Chateau of the Countess.—The Gossips.—The Farmer and his Neddy.—Sudden arrival and mysterious conduct of Carwin.—Therese relates the story of her persecutions.—Preparations for the Marriage of the Count and the Orphan.—Villanous offers of the Advocate.—Therese denounced a condemned Felon.

ACT 2, The Farm House and Pavilion.—Flight of the Orphan.—Dreadful machinations of the Advocate.—The Oath of Silence.—The Storm.—Interview of the Count and Therese.—Destruction of the Pavilion with Lightning. —Assassination of the Countess.—The Orphan of Geneva accused of Murder.

ACT 3, Agony of the Count.—Distress of Therese, and Benevolence of the Pastor.—Arrest of the Advocate.— Matrimonial Squabbles.—Friendship of the Farmer.—Examination of Carwin.—Address of the Pastor.—Awful Summons.—The Ordeal.—Despair and Confession of the Assassin—**GRAND DENOUEMENT.**

A COMIC SONG BY MR. MONTAGUE.

After which an entirely Original Laughable Farce by the REV. T. P. JENKINS, called

THE DILEMMA, OR, THE CAT IN A BAG.

Old Testy	Mr. PLATT.	Harbottle	Mr. MONTAGUE.
Bumper	Mr. HEAL.	Charles	Mr. MERCER.
Giles		Mr. REID.	
Jennet	Miss MERCER.	Betty	Miss SHEERER.

A COMIC SONG BY MR. REID.
A DUET BY MR. & MISS MERCER.

The whole to conclude with the Laughable Farce of

The Dead Shot.

Hector Timid	Mr. REID.	Thornton	Mr. MONTAGUE.	Williams	Mr. HEAL.
Captain Cannon	Mr. PLATT.		Wiseman	Mr. MERCER.	
Louisa Lovetrick	Mrs. REID.	Chatter (her Maid)	Miss SHEERER.		

Prices of Admission—Boxes, 2s. 6d.—Front Seats, 2s.—P'
CHILDREN under Ten Years of Age, Half-Price.

Doors open at half-past SIX, and to commence at SEVEN o'Clock.

TICKETS to be had of Mrs. REID.—WYNDHAM-ARMS, and of Mr. JO

Mr. REID's, Collection of Songs are now ready and can be had of Mr. R. at Mr. P' Monmouth and Glamorgan Bank.

JOHN G. BIRD, PRINTER, &c., BRIDGEND.

81 Two days after the production of 'Married Life' etc. (see 74) the above programme was offered 'For the Benefit of Mrs Reid' who would have been a member of the repertory company

82 Members of the ancient order of Rechabites from Bridgend on an outing to Southerndown, *c.*1903

83 The cast of the operetta 'The birth of the Union Jack' given in 1907 by members of the English Congregational Church under the baton of William Leyshon

84 A very crowded Dunraven Place on the occasion of Queen Victoria's Diamond Jubilee celebrations in 1897. Addressing the gathering is Mr McGaul, a prominent local businessman

85 The coronation of King George VI in 1937 was an occasion for national rejoicing. The country had passed through some grim years of depression and unemployment. Here, in common with thousands of ordinary people, the folk of Cheltenham Terrace and Suffolk Street forget their troubles and celebrate

86 A group of children and a patriotically decorated window in Cheltenham Terrace mark the 1937 coronation

87 The Right Honourable David Lloyd George breaks a journey at Bridgend during the First World War to address a gathering outside the Railway Station

88 The scene in Dunraven Place on the occasion of the unveiling of the War Memorial on Armistice Day 1921

89/90/91/92 St David's Day celebrations (1913 this page, 1921 opposite). Pupils of Penybont Boys' School mark the day when the streets are full of Norman lords and Welsh resistance leaders rubbing shoulders with the lossin-selling women of Kidwelly; when Ifor Bach lunges his wooden sword and parries a Norman attack with his three-ply shield; when daffodils grow out of buttonholes and pinned shawls, and earthy leeks proclaim the Welsh heritage. And when the battles have been won, the songs sung and the Dragon flutters from a broomstick mast, the anticipation and the joy of a half-holiday!

93 The day the first Prince of Wales comes into his own — 1 March 1920. It is a far cry from Caernarfon Castle to Penybont School yard, but the intention and the spirit remained the same

94 Not a demonstration of pupil-power or a take-over of the town but Ifor Bach, Caradog, Llywelyn and many a Norman baron and his lady from Bridgend (Penybont) Board School on Dydd Gwyl Dewi 1920 outside the Town Hall

95 At the Royal National Eisteddfod of Wales in Bridgend 1948. Two prominent local figures, Archdruid Wil Ifan and Rhys Williams (senr.), meet at a Gorsedd ceremony when Mr Williams was welcomed as a member of the Gorsedd in the picturesque setting of Newbridge Fields

96 Members of the then recently-formed Rotary Club of Bridgend with some of their ladies attending the Llandrindod Conference in 1926. The president, R. Horrocks, and vice-president, Canon Phillips, are seated immediately behind the shield

97 Councillor H. P. Williams, Chairman of Bridgend Urban District Council, reads the proclamation of the accession to the throne of Queen Elizabeth II on the steps of the Town Hall, February 1952

Trade

98　This business in Caroline Street is one of the oldest in the town. It was originally opened in the 1850s. In 1896 the grandfather of the present owner, A. J. Stokes, purchased the business from Mr East (see sign above shop). Standing in the entrance are Mr Richards, manager, and a counter assistant

99 An unidentified family and their 'front room shop' *c.*1905, of which there were so many. It is included as an excellent example of the dress and the business of the period

101 Bananas must have been a fast-selling line judging from the number on display outside this shop in Wyndham Street. The shop was established in the 19th century. In the years following the Second World War a popular restaurant, the Red Dragon, was opened on the first floor. Both shop and restaurant have now been replaced by Pauls

100   In 1910 you could buy a pound of apples for 1d and melons were 2½d or 3d in Robert Roberts' Caroline Street shop. The business was carried on by his son, C. Benson Roberts, until his retirement. The premises are now occupied by Tele-Electrical Services

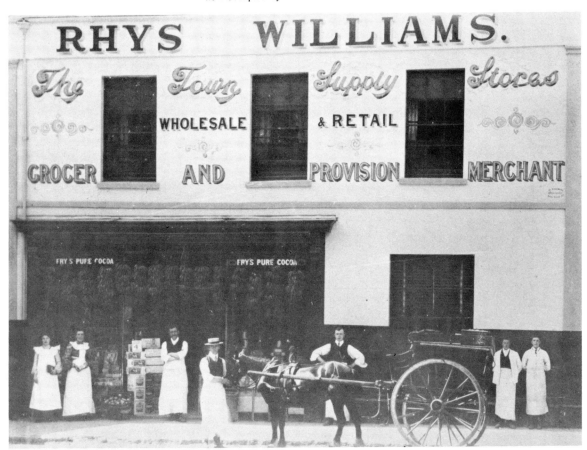

July the 18

Soles 10 Rabbits 1/2 Currants 2 flower 5½ Sugar 9 Goose 2 Mutton 18   0 : 7 : 0½

Peas 4 Sugar 1/2 Bread 1½ Pepper 2½ Butter 9 Po: 8 Lemons 6 Fish 6   0 : 3 : 6

& Veal 2/6 alder Flowers 6 grinding 4 Washing 1/6 Renceing 1/4 Sorning 1/6 Peas   0 : 8 : 0

Bean 9   0 : 0 : 9

Piece of Beef 12 Po: 3/6 Leg of Lambe 4 Po 1 Loin of Mutton 8 Po: 1/3   0 : 5 : 9

Brest of Veal 9 & a half 1/9 0 Lambs head 9 Fish 8 6 Pidgeons 1 0.0   0 : 3 : 11

kidney beans 2 Salt 9 Oatmeal 9 Cheese 6 Eggs 6 Butter 5 Po: 2/11   0 : 4 : 8

Bread 1 Peas 9 Milk 10½   0 : 1 : 6½

                         1 : 15 : 0

July 25

Cowcumber 1½ Coffee 11 Spirits of wine 10 fullerscarth 2 Sugar 9½   0 : 2 : 8

yest 1½ Beans 6 Snuff 1/4½ Turpentine 4 Flower ½ kidney 2½   0 : 3 : 00

Peas 4 Beskits 6 Bread 1 Coffee 11 Veal 1/8 Mutton 1/6   0 : 5 : 0

Peas 8 kidney beans 2½ Lambs 6 yest 1   0 : 1 : 5½

Round of Beef 25 Po: 6/9 Shoulder 11 Po: 2/3 Leg of Mutton 9 Po: 1/9   0 : 10 : 9

Lamb 1/5 Fish 9 half a dozen Pidgeons 1 Chicken Cowcombers 3   0 : 3 : 10

Milk Pot 2½ Salt 4½ Lemons 6½ Baskit 4 Eggs 8   0 : 1 : 11½

Butter 3/3 Wheate 5/4 Milk 10½   0 : 9 : 5½

                         1 : 18 : 1½

August the 1

grinding 4 Veal 1/8 Currants 2 Sugar 9½ Bread 3 Butter one Po: 8½   0 : 3 : 9

Peas 6 kidney beans 2 Iseinglass 8 Coten 1½ Bread 6 Cheese 6   0 : 2 : 5½

Butter 4 Calves head 1/1 Quarter Lamb 9 Fish 1/2½ naples 2   0 : 4 : 9½

Brest of Veal 2/6 Pidgeons half a dozen 1/3 Fish 1/10 Flower 8½   0 : 6 : 0½

Lemons 4 kidney beans 2 Bread 4 Cream 6 Tea 1 Sugar 9 Currants 3½   0 : 3 : 2½

Natmegs 1½ Eggs 9 Butter 5 Po: 2/11 Sugar 8 Milk 10 Coffee 8½   0 : 5 : 11½

                         1 : 6 : 0

102   A page from the household accounts of Mrs Elizabeth Martin who lived at Verville, Merthyrmawr, and died aged 78 in 1783. The page shown covers three weeks in 1763

103 The approach to Station Road at the turn of the century. The *Railway Inn* is without its additional storey; the building on the right is the Ruskin Photographic Studio

104 The junction of Wyndham Street and Derwen Road, formerly known as Oak and Ash Lane. The brick building behind the man on the left was the public weighbridge

105 It has been claimed that the Cattle Market was originally held at the corner of the present Wyndham Street and Adare Street on the site occupied by Lloyds Bank. Another site, known as the Shambles, was the area at the approach to the 15th-century bridge now occupied by Clay Travel Service. This photograph taken in 1933 shows the market at its penultimate location, now the Bus Station. The removal of the market to a site between Quarella Road and Brewery Lane marked its last move prior to its transfer to Cowbridge in 1977

106 E. Beasant, railway 'outside porter' and haulier, with his horse-drawn van outside Bridgend Railway Station, *c*.1906

107 Woodward's delivery van in Oak and Ash Lane, *c*.1914. Other business premises visible are Loosemore's hay, corn and chaff stores, and that of Mossford, sculptor

108   This building was the *Bear Hotel*, Dunraven Place, in the early years of the 20th century. It later provided accommodation for the Cleopatra Studio and when this photograph was taken was evidently serving as committee rooms for William Brace, who served as a Member of Parliament for a number of years. One of the burning issues of the election, 'Peers or People?', is displayed on one of the posters

109 An extract from the household accounts of Mrs G. Verity, Church Road, Bridgend, during a week in October, 1913. The goods were purchased from David Williams & Sons

110 The *Welcome to Town* inn, Nolton Street, at the end of the 19th century. Standing in the doorway is Mrs Mary Ann Thomas (née Llewellyn)

111/112 The *Dunraven Arms* hotel photographed in the early 1900s. It was built by Thomas Morgan. The lounge is an excellent example of the furnishing of the period. The *Dunraven Arms* was built on the site of another inn, the *Oak and Ash*. The street on the left hand side was known as Coity Road but is now Derwen Road — a possible link with the *Oak and Ash* as Derwen is Welsh for oak

113 Officers of the Bridgend Fat Stock Show 1927. (Left to right) D. J. Gwyn, W. H. Jones, H. E. Taylor, J. P. Maitland, Sir Rhys Williams, Bart., G. Jenkins and Hopkin D. Morgan

114 Bridgend Traders' Outing 1922. Among the company were such well-known names as John Lewis, David Stradling, Evan David, Clifford Anthony and Rhys Williams, father and son

. . JONES' . .

High-class Fancy Repository

Leather Goods, Doulton and Worcester China,
Fancy Jewellery, Art Needlework.

Dispensing of Prescriptions a Speciality.

J. Jones, PHARMACEUTICAL . . CHEMIST, . .
BRIDGEND.

Drugs and Chemicals of guaranteed purity.
Surgical Appliances. Photographic Materials

115/116/117   Some of the shops trading in Bridgend in 1910. Taken from a contemporary guide book

The Old Post Office, ✤ BRIDGEND.
W. H. Thomas,
Bookseller, Bookbinder, Stationer, Fancy Goods
—Dealer, Tobacconist.—

The Best Local Views and Heraldic China.   Smokers' Requisites.

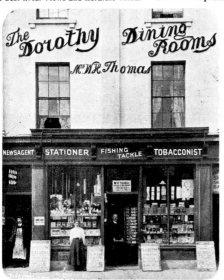

The Dorothy Dining Rooms
First Floor.   ::   Side Entrance.

Well-Appointed Dining & Tea Rooms.

QUICK SERVICE. :: GOOD COOKING.
MODERATE CHARGES.

Mrs. W. H. THOMAS, Proprietress.

"Refresh Yourself at the 'CAFÉ ROYAL.'"

W. H. JOHN,
Baker, Confectioner and Caterer.

CAFE ROYAL, DUNRAVEN PLACE,
Machine Bakery, Riverside,
BRIDGEND.

Bread delivered to all parts of the town and district daily.
Marquees on Hire.
Nat. Tel. 0183.   Telegrams: JOHN, CAFE ROYAL.

"We all eat Bread. Why not eat the Best?"

Do You know this Shop?

No doubt you do know it — in a way — because you may pass it occasionally; but you might pass it every day and yet not "know" it in the best sense of the word.

This is one of the shops which to know is to appreciate. In every line the value offered is decidedly on the customer's side, and in Drugs and Medicines the quality is so high as to bring a sense of security to the buyer. This safety is both real and valuable. You need it.

E. T. RICH, M.P.S.

Dispensing . . .	Personal attention. Customers can rely on having their Prescriptions accurately dispensed with the best of Drugs.
Sick Room and Toilet Requisites.	A full assortment always kept in stock at lowest prices.
Photography . .	Cameras from 5/- upwards. Plates, Films, and P.O.P., &c., fresh weekly. Developing and printing promptly attended to.
Garden Seeds .	That grow. These are the kind that we sell.
Patent Medicines	At Store Prices.

SPECIALITIES

"WILLIAMS (PONTARDAWE) WORM LOZENGES," 9½d., 1/1½ and 2/9
"BRONCURO," for Coughs, 1 1½   "SCAMMONY PILLS," 1/- and 2 6
"TICURO," for Neuralgia, 1/1½   "FINBERG" MALT and OIL,
"INHALIT," for Colds - 10½d.   1/3 and 2/3
"WAUKWEL," for Corns - 7½d.   "FINBERG" EMULSION,
                                  1 -, 1/10 and 2/6

BUSINESS HOURS—8.30 a.m. to 8 p.m.
Wednesdays, 2 p.m. ; Saturdays, 10.30 p.m.

RICH, The Chemist, Bridgend.
AND AT 30 HIGH STREET, SWANSEA.

P.O. 'Phone 25.   Telegrams : RICH, BRIDGEND.

118 This chemist's shop has had a 'face-lift' since 1910 as customers of G. Trenberth, the present proprietor, will testify

119 'Bridgend's Premier Laundry' in 1910. When the Rhiw developments started, this building, which stood on part of the present multi-storey car park, was demolished with other old buildings

For Excellence of Colours and Finish send to

The Victoria Hygienic Laundry

(GWYN NICHOLLS & WINFIELD, Ltd.),

BRIDGEND'S Premier Laundry.

Works also at Llandaff and Neath.

A1 Shirt and Collar Dressers, and General Laundrymen.
Ladies' Finery a Speciality.   Dry Cleaners.

THE MOST UP-TO-DATE LAUNDRY IN THE DISTRICT.

In the foreground of the photo of our Shirt and Collar Department is to be seen a machine for Automatically Dampening the Seams of Collars to obviate the cracking at the edges; and another for Folding, Shaping, and imparting a Smooth :: Finish to the whole length of the Collar. ::

Our Vans visit Bridgend, Porthcawl, Pyle, Kenfig Hill, Southerndown, Pencoed, Cowbridge, Pontycymmer, Nantymoel, Maesteg, Caerau and districts.

120 The staff of Miles' bakery which, when this picture was taken in 1918, was situated in Market Street on a site now occupied by the Bridgend Printing Company's retail shop

GIVE US A TRIAL !   National Telephone 57 Bridgend.

London House, Bridgend,

March 18 1867

J. C. Nichol Esqr.

Sir

I am desired to request the favor of your attendance as complimentary Mourner at the Funeral of the late Miss Turberville of Ewenny Abbey on Friday next the 22nd inst to Ewenny the place of interment.

An early answer will oblige.

Yours obediently,

C Thos Hughes,

Undertaker.

P.S. You will much oblige by being at the Abbey not later than 11 o'Clock.

121 This mourning card is a reminder that during the last century and before the advent of modern undertakers and American-styled morticians, drapers were responsible for 'funerals completely furnished'

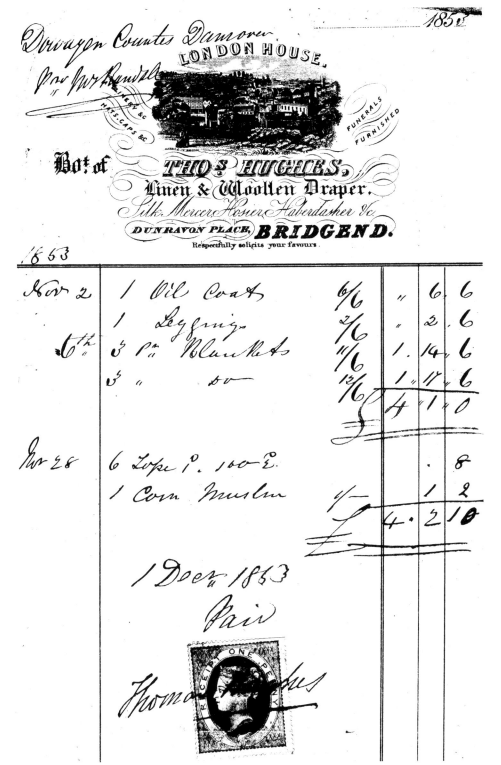

Dowager Countess Dunraven
Pro Mr Randall

LONDON HOUSE.

LINEN &c
HATS·CAPS &c

FUNERALS FURNISHED

Bot of **THOS HUGHES,**
Linen & Woollen Draper,
Silk Mercer Hosier Haberdasher &c

DUNRAVON PLACE, **BRIDGEND.**

Respectfully solicits your favours.

1853

1853					
Nov 2	1 Oil Coat	6/6	"	6	6
	1 Leggings	2/6	"	2	6
6th	3 Pr Blankets	11/6	1	14	6
	3 " do	13/6	1 "	17 "	6
			4 "	1 "	0
Nov 28	6 Tape 1d 100 E.		.		8
	1 Corn Muslin	1/—		1	2
			4 .	2	10

1 Decr 1853
Paid

Thomas Hughes

122   The close connection of the Earl of Dunraven's family with the town, as is evident in such street names as Wyndham, Adare, Mount Earl and Dunraven Place, may also be seen in the support given to local tradesmen through the agent to the Earl — John Randall. Note the different spelling of Dunraven — a printer's error or a reference to the River Ogmore flowing past the rear of the shop?

Bought by _____ Bridgend _____ 186

Of **C. E. Perry,**

CONFECTIONER,

Bread & Fancy Biscuit Baker

DDING CAKES. TWELFTH NIGHT CHARACTERS &c.

EWENNY SHOP. THE TEA POT SHOP.

BRIDGEND AND MAESTEG

18

Agent for Huntley & Palmers Reading Biscuits.

LONDON HOUSE,

Dunraven Place, Bridgend, 18

M

Bought of W. J. Lewis,

(late Hughes)

LINEN & WOOLLEN DRAPER,

Accounts Rendered Midsummer & Christmas

FUNERALS FURNISHED

2½ Per cent charged on overdue Accounts

JOUR FOLIO

Stephens & Hawkins Bristol

Memo from **Edward Hughes**

General Draper and Silk Mercer.

Bridgend, Glam.

London House,

London House
34 E. HUGHES 32
OUTFITTING MILLINERY E.HUGHES GENERAL DRAPERY

WALKEY THOMAS &C? CARDIFF

To _____ 19____

123/124/125/126/127 A selection of the attractive bill-heads favoured by tradesmen in the 19th century

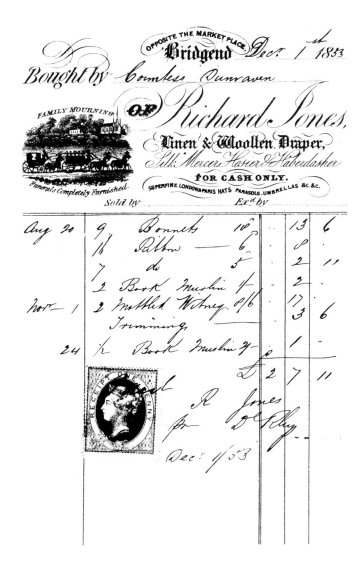

OPPOSITE THE MARKET PLACE

Bridgend Dec. 1st 1853

Bought by Countess Dunraven

FAMILY MOURNING

OF **Richard Jones,**

Linen & Woollen Draper,

Silk Mercer Hosier & Haberdasher

FOR CASH ONLY.

SUPERFINE LONDON & PARIS HATS PARASOLS UMBRELLAS &C &C.

Funerals Completely Furnished

Sold by   Ex.d by

Aug 20	9	Bonnets	10°		13	6
	1½	Ribbon	6°		8	
	7	do	5°		2	11
	½	Book Muslin 4			2	
Nov 1	2	Mottled Witney 8/6			17	3	6
		Trimmings			3	6
	24	½	Book Muslin 2/		1	
			£	2	7	11

RECEIPT ONE PENNY

R Jones
for D Rhy

Dec. 1/53

Spring & Summer Novelties, 1907.

Per BOOK POST.

BRIDGEND AP 13 07

Mrs. *Jones*

Windmill Drid

Porthcawl

Or Occupier.

E. HUGHES, LONDON HOUSE, BRIDGEND.

128/129 What the well-dressed Edwardian lady was wearing in 1907. An example of the advertising material despatched to customers

E. HUGHES, London House, BRIDGEND,

Begs to announce that his SHOW ROOMS are now replete with the

Latest Novelties

• • •

for the

SPRING & SUMMER SEASONS,

and requests the favour of an early visit.

DRESS FABRICS.
MANTLES,
JACKETS,
COATS,
BLOUSES,
COSTUMES,
SKIRTS,
CORSETS,
UNDERCLOTHING.

MILLINERY,
FLOWERS, FEATHERS,
HOSIERY, GLOVES,
LACE GOODS, &c.

130 London House, general drapers and outfitters, has figured prominently in the business life of the town since the year of Trafalgar, 1805. Since 1900 the business has been owned by the Hughes family and the recent closure of the shop marked the end of one of the oldest business premises in the town. This photograph was taken in 1904

131 This is the first branch of W. H. Smith, the well-known booksellers and stationers, to be opened in Bridgend. The *Glamorgan Gazette* office now occupies the site on which this shop stood. The manager in the entrance is D. J. Davies, father of Leslie Davies who has continued his father's business as newsagent at the shop in the Bus Station

132 The fleet of vehicles and parade of animals at Ellaway's bakery, Riverside. Delivery may not have been very speedy but it was reliable. This bakery transferred its operations from premises in Mackworth Street

133 Members of the staff and the steam-driven delivery vehicle of Stiles Brewery, Tondu Road, *c*.1897

BOARD'S GARAGE, BRIDGEND.

·:· PHONE 156 ·:·

J. P. BOARD & CO. AUSTIN CARS

GARAGE

J.P.BOARD+CO.

MORRIS CARS.

Sales & Service Depôt for Morris & Austin Cars. Garage Accomodation for 300 Cars.

PHOTO, HARRY JONES, NEATH.

134/135 (Above) the second premises in town to be occupied by Board's garage, *c*.1924, the first having been opened in 1918 on the site later occupied by Woolworths. Of interest is the fact that they are among the oldest agents for Morris cars in the country. (Below) the demolition of the premises seen above, prior to the building of the present modern, attractive garage

136 A Wednesday afternoon (early closing day) in Adare Street. The bunting and flags are hung as part of the town's celebrations of the coronation of King George VI

Religion, Education
and Public Services

137   The present church of St Mary's, Nolton, is modern, dating from 1887. It replaced an ancient building
which was the former chapel-of-ease of the church at Coity. The spire and its supporting tower were added in
1898 as gifts to the church. This photograph was taken c.1900

138/139 Adjoining a 12th-century castle at the top of Newcastle Hill stands St Illtyd's Church, known in earlier times as St Leonard's. It was largely reconstructed in the 19th century when the north aisle was added. It is claimed that the communion plate is early 17th-century. In the early years of this century the chancel was enlarged

140 The Meeting House at the foot of Newcastle Hill ranks among the oldest chapels in the district being established in 1717 and rebuilt in 1795. The chapel figures prominently in the early history of non-conformity in Glamorgan

141 Tabernacle Chapel in Adare Street 'grew' out of the Meeting House 'for Protestant Dissenters'. The first or old Tabernacle was built in Elder Street in 1810. This is now the site of the Tabernacle Hall. The present building was started in 1850 and completed in the following year

142/143 Work proceeding on the present Hope Baptist Chapel in 1906. Previously members had worshipped in Queen Street since 1850 in a chapel built on the site now occuped by Gilesports. The total cost of the new, spacious chapel exceeded £5,000

144 Following a successful mission conducted in the town in 1905 — the year of the last great religious revival in Wales — a difference of opinion arose between the minister of Ruhamah Welsh Baptist Church and some of the members. So acute was this difference and so insoluble the problems that the relationship of pastor with his flock was terminated in 1906. With a number of his principal supporters Mr Jones established a new English Baptist cause, taking the name Christ Church

145/146 A view of St Mary's, Nolton, prior to the addition of the spire in 1898. The church has some beautiful features notably the Italian-style reredos and, of course, the spire which, like the tower and surmounting cross of Newcastle church, is a prominent landmark and constant reminder of the work and witness of Christianity in the town

147 St Mary's, Nolton, church fete and bazaar *c.*1930. Included in this group are Canon David Phillips, Mrs Rees Williams, the mother of Lord Ogmore, and Miss E. Booker of Slon, Ogmore-by-Sea (now *Sea Lawns* hotel)

148 (Overleaf) In an era when the internal combustion engine had not enslaved society and movement from one's native heath was a rare occurrence the annual Sunday School trip was the event of the year. Our photograph shows scholars of Tabernacle Chapel Sunday School with their friends and relations at Ogmore-by-Sea. The journey was undertaken by horse-drawn wagonettes or 'breaks' as they were more popularly known

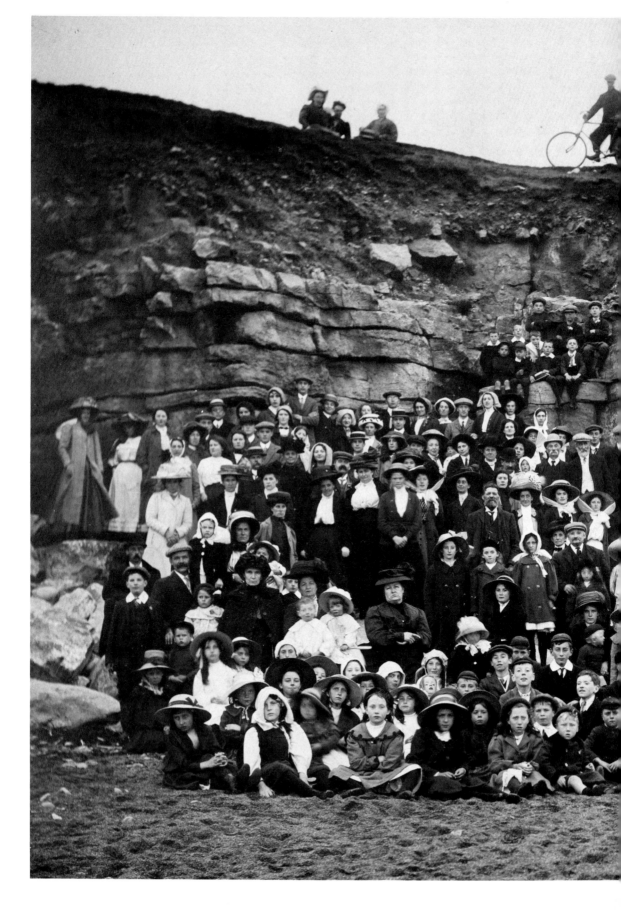

149 John Rankin (seated in centre), the first headmaster of Bridgend County School, was appointed in 1896. This group photograph of the staff was taken on Mr Rankin's retirement in 1928

150 In 1935 the County School for Boys occupied a new school in Ewenny Road. With the headmaster, W. E. Thomas, and his deputy, Steve Jenkins, are a number of staff who were to give long and distinguished service to the school. Among them are T. Bevan, A. Hesling and W. Haydn Jones who was to succeed W. E. Thomas

151 Bryntirion Preparatory School for Boys was founded in 1924 by Rev. N. H. Parcell, seated centre. In this 1930 group a future Medical Officer of Health (Dr Ian Peebles) and a Crown Court judge (Peter Hopkin-Morgan) appear among the boys

152/153 Penybont Primary (formerly Bridgend Board) School, Quarella Road. The centenary of its foundation was celebrated in 1977. Through the century the name of the school has been changed on a number of occasions. Today the old building accommodates the Welsh School (Ysgol Gymraeg Penybont) and the Penybont Infants School. (Below) the cookery class of the Girls' School in March 1925

PENYBONT GIRLS' SCHOOL, COOKERY CLASS.   MARCH. 1925.

154/155 (Above) Penybont Infants' School with staff, March 1925; (below) Penybont Boys' School, standard IV, March 1925, with their teacher, E. T. Griffiths

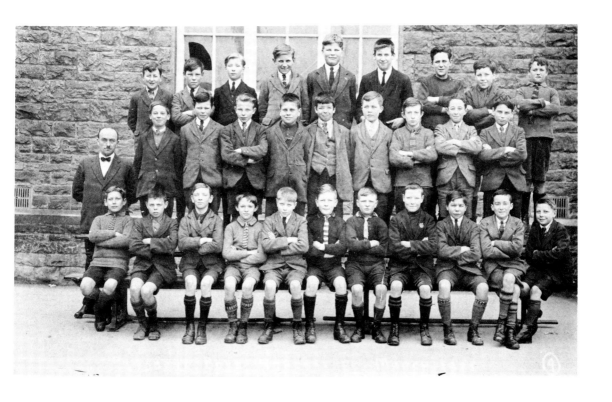

156 From surviving minutes of the National School we gather that by 1824 new buildings to accommodate a new school were being used on a site adjoining Nolton Street in what is now known as Free School Court

157 Oldcastle Infants' School with staff, 1914. This, the second elementary school in town, was built to serve pupils in the southern and eastern districts

158 The demand for labour in Bridgend and district attracted large numbers of Irish immigrants in the wake of the 'hungry forties'. Consequently in 1855 this Roman Catholic church and school was built on land in Ewenny Road

159 This was the Bridgend Preparatory and Commercial School the principal of which (inset) was Rev. T. Gwilym Jones. The school stood in Sunnyside until it was demolished to make way for the inner by-pass road

160 Officers and committee of Bridgend and District Welsh Society (Cymdeithas y Cymrodorion Penybont a'r Cylch) 1932. Among prominent Bridgend citizens are T. Bevan, E. T. Owen, Miss Mason and Tudor Griffiths

161 The old wing of Bridgend General Hospital, formerly the Bridgend and Cowbridge Union Workhouse, built 1836/37. Part was used to accommodate the police in 1841

162 In 1864 a lunatic asylum was built at Angelton, two miles outside Bridgend. In the course of time buildings have been extended and the institution enlarged. These buildings and those at the former Parcgwyllt have been renamed and form a unified mental hospital

163 An early 1920s version of a Dennis fire engine belonging to Bridgend Fire Brigade seen on Ewenny Bridge

164 Members of the 1st Bridgend Troop of Boy Scouts at the All-Wales Scout Camp held at Margam in 1928 and attended by Sir Robert Baden-Powell, Chief Scout. In the group are Cecil Jones, James Emery, Ernest Carver and Scoutmaster F. Rouse

165   The 4th Bridgend (St Mary's, Nolton) Girl Guides in 1930. The Division Commander was
Mrs H. J. Randall

166 Contingent of Boy Scouts (Hope Chapel) seen in front of the chapel

Men in Uniform

167   Bridgend was a flourishing centre of the Volunteer force. In 1895 there were two companies of Volunteer infantry well over strength and one company of artillery even more over strength. Our photograph shows the 1st Coy. (Bridgend) Volunteer Regiment with the Battalion Cup won on 25 November 1886

168 The background is familiar — the Square, now Dunraven Place, with D. Verity's house on the extreme right — but we have no record of the company of militiamen or volunteers. Taken in the 1870s it is the oldest photograph in the book

169 Officers and N.C.O's of the Glamorgan Yeomanry, Bridgend, c.1897

170 A later (1896) photograph of the 1st Coy. Volunteer Regiment. The large figure seated second from the right is Sgt. T. Williams (the *Bear*), great grandfather of Ernest Carver, the well-known photographer

171 Bridgend Detachment, D Company, 1st Battalion Glamorgan Volunteer Regiment. This was the winning section at the Glamorgan Open Competition in rifle-shooting at Newton Camp, Porthcawl, September 1917

172 As part of a national drive to promote the sale of War Savings Certificates tanks of the First World War toured the country. This was the scene in Dunraven Place on 8 June 1918 when 'Egbert', a Cambrai tank, appeared

Bridgend
Staatliche Munitionsfabrik

Länge (westl. Greenw.) 3 33 25   Breite 51 30 08
Mißweisung — 12 04' (Mitte 1940)   Zielhöhe über NN 30 m

Maßstab etwa 1 : 37 500

Geost   Am

Karte 1 100 00

GB/E 26

173 A German Luftwaffe reconnaissance photograph dated 24 August 1940 showing the Royal Ordnance Factory, Waterton, and part of the town. The factory was constructed in two distinct sections, one for storing munitions and the other as a shell-filling factory. Fortunately it escaped being bombed during the war

174 In February 1941 the Air Ministry formed the Air Training Corps as a pre-training unit of the R.A.F. Bridgend County School was among the first to form a school unit. Later, with other Flights, the School Flight was merged to become 1092 Squadron

175 A detachment of Special Constables who served in the town during the Second World War. The 'regular' officer is P.C. David (Dai) Pugh

176 Part of Island Farm Camp, Bridgend, the famous Second World War P.O.W. camp from which in the final months of the war 67 German officers, including U-boat commanders and SS men, escaped through a tunnel causing panic and excitement before they were all recaptured within a week

ACKNOWLEDGEMENTS

I would like to thank the following for giving their kind permission to use their photographs:

Peter Board (133, 134); Bridgend R.F.C. (47, 48, 49); Ernest Carver (2, 18, 34, 39, 75, 79, 103, 140, 164, 165, 166, 167, 170, 172); Mrs V. David (43, 44); Leslie Davies (131); Mrs Hazel Evans (9, 10, 11); *Glamorgan Gazette* (5, 23, 24, 37, 46, 56, 60, 61, 85, 96, 99, 135, 157, 162); E. T. Griffiths (89, 90, 91, 92, 93, 94, 154, 155, 160); John Howell (25); E. T. O. Hughes (121, 122, 123-127, 128, 129, 130); Mrs D. Elwyn James (26, 87, 159); Mrs F. M. Jones (6, 14); Mrs K. Jones (55); Mrs W. Haydn Jones (51, 52, 53, 54, 58, 59, 65, 66, 67, 149, 150, 174); E. B. Lewis (57, 62, 68); Mid Glamorgan County Library (1, 3, 4, 12, 13, 15, 16, 19, 20, 28, 29, 30, 31, 32, 33, 35, 45, 50, 63, 64, 69, 80, 82, 88, 97, 104, 106, 107, 108, 110, 115, 116, 117, 118, 119, 132, 136, 137, 138, 139, 141, 142, 143, 144, 145, 146, 147, 151, 152, 158, 161, 163, 171, 173, 175, 176); Robert Morgan (105, 113); Mrs E. Pullman (86, 120, 153); Mrs G. Rees (76, 77); C. Benson Roberts (78, 83, 100); South Glamorgan County Libraries (27, 36, 156); A. J. Stokes (98); Tabernacle Church (148); Chris Taylor (38, 40, 41, 42); Mrs Florence Thomas (7, 8, 84, 169); D. Verity (74, 81, 102, 109, 168); Owain Williams (17, 21, 22, 95, 101, 111, 112, 114); Dr Peter R. J. Williams (70, 71, 72, 73).

My thanks are also due to R. W. Davies, County Librarian, Mid Glamorgan, and his staff, especially David J. Pearce, for their interest and support; Mrs Pat Hurley of the *Glamorgan Gazette*; also to well-known local photographer Ernest Carver whose technical advice and generous co-operation have been invaluable. Many people, too numerous to mention, have offered information and advice. To them I tender my warm appreciation.

D.G.W.